AUDREY HEPBURN

For Bill Hess,
my father.

Just like Audrey,
your greatest gift is
how you make others feel.

AUDREY HEPBURN

THE ILLUSTRATED WORLD OF A FASHION ICON

Megan Hess

Hardie Grant

BOOKS

CONTENTS

INTRODUCTION

Audrey Hepburn stole hearts on screen and off with her unconventional looks, innate sense of performance and effortless charm. She was also a bone fide fashion icon, with a trademark simplicity that is now the definition of classic.

DURING THE FILM INDUSTRY'S GOLDEN ERA, a time when Hollywood was bursting with stars, Audrey was a unique and captivating presence. She was one of the most in-demand actors for decades — appearing in some of the greatest movies of all time, collecting a raft of awards and practically guaranteeing box office success.

Muse to legendary photographers Richard Avedon and Cecil Beaton, and a regular on the covers of *Vogue* and *Harper's Bazaar*, Audrey is also forever linked to the world of high fashion, especially the career of her close friend and couture master Hubert de Givenchy. The opening scene of *Breakfast at Tiffany's*, where Holly Golightly in a Givenchy gown steps out of a taxi onto the deserted Fifth Avenue pavement to gaze into the Tiffany's front window, is one of cinema's most famous fashion moments. It is just one of the many unforgettable looks Audrey brought to the silver screen in collaboration with Givenchy.

But the darling of 1950s Hollywood was so much more than just a glamorous movie star with a coveted look. Audrey was also deeply touched by her childhood experience of war and spent years of her life training to be a dancer, which instilled in her an immense strength, work ethic, empathy and thoughtfulness. She dedicated her later life to the service of others, as a devoted mother of her two sons and as a UNICEF Goodwill Ambassador for humanitarian causes.

Audrey was undoubtedly one of the most recognisable women ever to grace our screens, but she left a lasting impression on the world off screen too – for her effortless style and unmatched character. She is truly worthy of her status as an icon.

THE
WOMAN

WITH HER UNDENIABLE STAR POWER and enviable style, Audrey Hepburn was Hollywood's leading lady of choice during the 1950s and '60s, epitomising the industry's glittering studio era. But she started life far from the lights of Tinseltown.

Born in Brussels to an English father and Dutch mother, Audrey spent her childhood years moving between Belgium, the United Kingdom and the Netherlands. Before she had reached adulthood, she could speak six languages and was a true citizen of the world. She had also lived through war, survived severe malnutrition and borne witness to some of the worst acts ever inflicted upon humanity.

Audrey's first and most enduring love was ballet. It was her dream to become a professional dancer and she worked hard to achieve it, but she was destined to light up the screen instead. After being discovered by chance on a small film set on the French Riviera aged twenty-two, she rose to fame with breathtaking speed.

Audrey Kathleen Ruston was born on
4 May 1929 in Brussels. She had two
half-brothers and a complex family
heritage. Her mother, Baroness Ella Van
Heemstra, was from Dutch nobility, and
her father, Joseph Ruston, was a British
citizen born in Austria-Hungary.

The name Hepburn, which Audrey
would adopt as a young adult, is a nod
to distant relatives on her father's side.

Audrey's early years were spent crisscrossing Europe.
She lived briefly in Belgium and the Netherlands with
her parents and brothers before being sent to boarding
school in the English countryside aged just six.

A shy child who preferred the company of books
and animals to people, Audrey later described
the move as a 'lesson in independence'.

Around this time, Joseph abruptly left
the family. Audrey adored her father and
took his departure hard.

But despite missing home and being devastated by her father's absence, Audrey's time at boarding school was happy for one key reason: she started taking dance classes from a London ballet master who travelled to the school in Kent to teach once a week.

It was the start of a lifelong love.

"

FOR ME THE only things of INTEREST ARE those linked to THE HEART.

"

Soon Audrey was on the move again.

In September 1939, Britain had
declared war on Germany and
Ella thought her daughter would
be safer back in the Netherlands.

They relocated to a sprawling estate
owned by Ella's family in Arnhem.

Audrey enrolled at school under
the name Edda Van Heemstra
and started to take all her lessons
in Dutch in order to disguise
her British roots amid growing
wartime suspicion.

For a while they lived comfortably in Arnhem. Audrey continued her ballet training and quickly built a reputation for being a determined and talented student.

In May 1940 the Sadler's Wells ballet company toured Europe and Audrey had tickets to their show in Arnhem. For the occasion, Ella had a long taffeta dress made for Audrey at great expense. After the performance, Audrey was called on stage to present the dancers with a spray of tulips and roses.

It would be one of the town's last free moments for years.

In 1940 Holland was invaded. The Nazi Party took over swiftly, and in the months that followed Audrey's family was stripped of all their wealth and began living under strict occupation.

By 1944, the Germans had blocked supply routes for food and fuel, leaving people to starve and freeze to death.

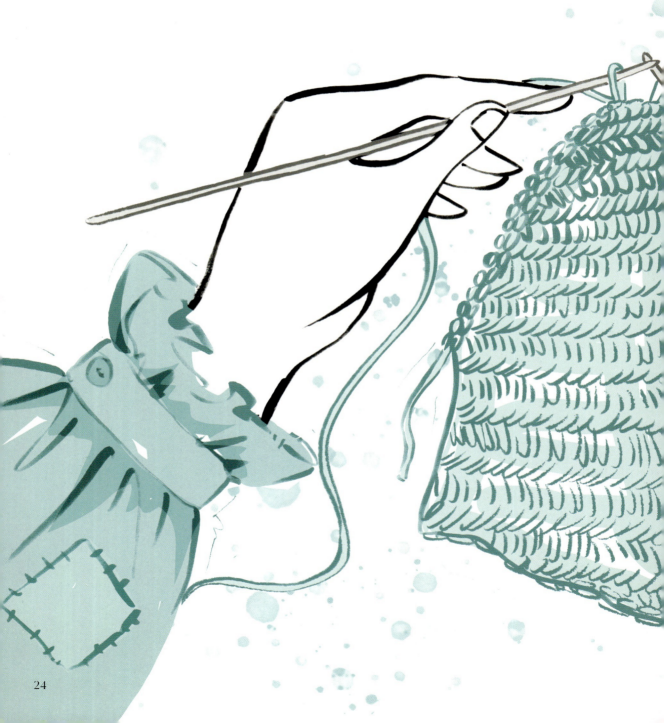

Despite increasingly harsh conditions,
Audrey maintained her love of ballet.

To distract herself from the worsening
food shortages and brutality, she gave
dancing lessons to younger students.

As it became harder to buy ballet clothes,
Audrey started dancing in makeshift shoes
sewn from felt that barely lasted a single
performance and her mother unpicked
old woollen jumpers to knit into tights.

"

THERE WAS A WAR,
but your dreams
FOR YOURSELF
go on.

I WANTED
to be a dancer.

"

Audrey also gave secret ballet performances to raise funds for the Dutch resistance. These invitation-only events were staged behind heavy blackout curtains, with lookouts stationed at all entrances, ready to warn of approaching German soldiers.

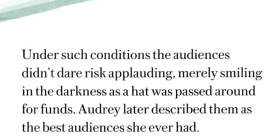

Under such conditions the audiences didn't dare risk applauding, merely smiling in the darkness as a hat was passed around for funds. Audrey later described them as the best audiences she ever had.

Audrey helped the resistance in other ways too. Being young, she was afforded some freedoms and was often called upon to deliver messages. She once resorted to stuffing copies of the tiny underground newspaper into her woollen socks in order to ride them across town undetected.

In the final days of the war, she risked her life to warn a British paratrooper who was hiding in the woods that he would likely be captured if he remained where he was.

She was picking wildflowers on her way out of the woods when she was met by a German soldier. Ever-charming even then, Audrey innocently handed over her bouquet of blooms before running back home to deliver the news that the Englishman would be at the secret location that night for safe housing.

UNITED NATIONS RELIEF

CHOCOLATE
CHOCOLATE
CHOCOLATE
CHOCOLATE

By the time Holland was liberated in 1945, sixteen-year-old Audrey was severely malnourished and had witnessed shocking acts of cruelty – she later said that 'the cold clutch of human terror' from that time never left her.

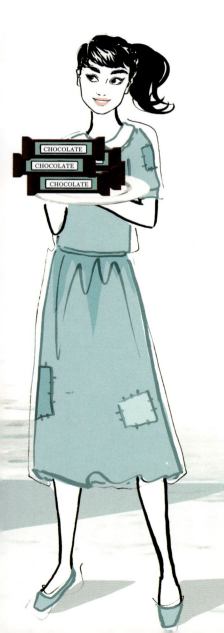

The day the United Nations Relief and Rehabilitation Administration came to administer aid, Audrey was given seven chocolate bars by a UN worker and ate them all at once.

She was promptly sick, but insisted that moment gave her an insatiable sweet tooth.

The true marvels of the aid operation were the boxes and boxes of supplies – food, blankets, medication and clothes – that filled schools and halls, ready to be handed out to people who needed them.

After years subsisting on almost nothing, it was a potent experience of charity that would remain with Audrey forever.

"

I BELIEVE IN being strong when EVERYTHING seems to be GOING WRONG.

"

As the horrors of war subsided, Audrey
and her mother found odd jobs in Arnhem
and Amsterdam to support themselves,
sharing the income between themselves.

Her mother took jobs as a florist, hotel
clerk and nanny, while Audrey worked
as a secretary, model and actor.

They also volunteered at a hospital
for soldiers wounded in the war.

But Audrey was not ready to
give up on her dream of dancing.

She and her mother moved to
England, where Audrey received a
scholarship with Ballet Rambert.

Audrey was full of hope for her ballet career
and worked hard to make up for lost time.

However, it soon became clear that
not only had she missed vital years of
training, she had been weakened by the
effects of prolonged malnutrition, and at
5 feet 7 inches, she was also considered
too tall for a dancer.

It was a devastating blow when her teacher
and mentor Madame Rambert told her that
she would never be a professional ballerina.

But a career on stage still beckoned,
and Audrey continued to audition for parts in
musicals and small films while modelling for
commercial photographers to pay the bills.

It was necessity — rather than any romantic
notion of stardom — that drove her to take
any modest job she could get.

In 1948 she made her official stage debut on the
West End as a chorus dancer in *High Button
Shoes.* Musical theatre wasn't her beloved
classical ballet, but she needed the work.

Despite her small part and a self-confessed
lack of skill for jazz dancing, she had an
irrepressible radiance on stage and loved
being in the theatre.

She was also developing her signature flair off stage. The lead dancer in *High Button Shoes* commented that Audrey had 'one skirt, one blouse, one pair of shoes and a beret.

'But she had fourteen scarves.

'What she did with them week by week, you wouldn't believe.'

"

WHEN I WEAR
a silk scarf
I NEVER FEEL

so definitely like
A WOMAN,
a beautiful woman.

"

The ballet dream wasn't completely lost. Audrey was cast in her first major role in a British film, chosen from a pool of thousands to play ballerina Nora Brentano in *Secret People*, a post-war political drama.

While happy to be back dancing, Audrey was far from convinced of her acting ability and leant heavily on the coaching and reassurance of her co-stars to get through the shoot.

REY

It was while shooting her next film, *Monte Carlo Baby*, on the French Riviera in 1951 that Audrey caught the eye of famed French author Colette.

Casting had begun for a Broadway adaptation of Colette's novel *Gigi*, but producers were having trouble finding a suitable leading lady.

Happening to pass the shoot on the way into her hotel, Colette saw Audrey from across the set, fooling around in a quiet moment between shoots.

Without knowing anything about Audrey, Colette was immediately captivated. 'Voilà ma Gigi!' she exclaimed.

And with that, Audrey was
on her way to Broadway.

From this unlikely beginning,
her star rose quickly once
she crossed the Atlantic.

Audrey

Audrey was a complete unknown when she arrived in New York for *Gigi*. Rehearsals for the musical were gruelling, and nobody was sure of Colette's choice of star — not least the star herself.

But reviews for the previews were gushing, and by the official opening night Audrey could barely get into her dressing room for the flowers.

Before the end of the show's first week, she had become the talk of the town and her name was up in lights.

The Broadway audiences
loved her, and before long
Hollywood came calling.

"

NOTHING
is impossible.
THE WORD ITSELF
says 'I'm possible'.

"

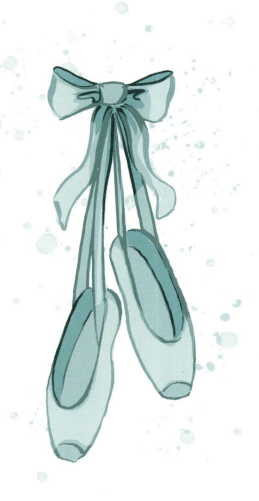

THE
WORK

WITHIN YEARS OF SIGNING with Paramount Pictures, Audrey would be one of the world's biggest stars. For the next two decades she worked almost constantly, making twenty-two films between 1951 and 1967, including legendary titles like *Roman Holiday*, *Funny Face* and *Breakfast at Tiffany's*, and winning scores of accolades.

Audrey also cemented herself as one of the great fashion muses of all time and built a lifelong friendship with designer Hubert de Givenchy. She shot with legendary photographers and single-handedly introduced a new standard of sophisticated style to audiences accustomed to the Hollywood bombshells of the day. Audrey's physique and manner made her the ideal fashion model, and her work as a model contributed significantly to her success as an actor. Her creative partnership with Givenchy was the first of its kind, pioneering the actor–designer relationship that continues today.

As her star grew and the awards started rolling in, she remained unconvinced of her own dramatic talents and entertained wistful hopes of leaving show business behind for a quieter life. Audrey chased love and happiness over success and fame, and even at the height of her career managed to stay true to the characteristics and values that made her unique.

Audrey's breakthrough film role was in the romantic comedy *Roman Holiday*, about a rebellious princess on a romp through the streets of the Italian capital.

Audrey was back in Europe for the shoot, staying at the luxurious Hotel Hassler at the top of the Spanish Steps.

The crowds that gathered to watch her and leading man Gregory Peck at iconic locations across the city made the days challenging and long, but she loved every minute of it.

Peck was biggest star in film at the time, but by the time the movie had screened – and achieved huge box office success – all anyone could talk about was Audrey.

It was on *Roman Holiday* that Audrey first worked with legendary costume designer Edith Head. At their first meeting, the unknown actor arrived at the seasoned designer's hotel room wearing a dark suit with white collar and cuffs. A sprig of white lily of the valley was in her buttonhole and a pair of white gloves completed her look.

'This was a girl way ahead of high fashion,' Edith said. 'She deliberately looked different from other women.'

Edith would later tell reporters Audrey knew more about fashion than any other actress she'd worked with – except maybe Marlene Dietrich.

Despite her newcomer status, Audrey had strong opinions about her wardrobe for *Roman Holiday*.

She politely refused to wear anything she didn't approve of and made significant changes to Edith's designs, insisting on simpler necklines, wider belts and flatter shoes.

The image of Princess Ann in a wide skirt, plain white shirt with sleeves rolled up and scarf breezily tied around her neck as she zooms around on a Vespa became a cultural touchstone.

"

CLOTHES
always give me a
GREAT DEAL
of self-confidence.

"

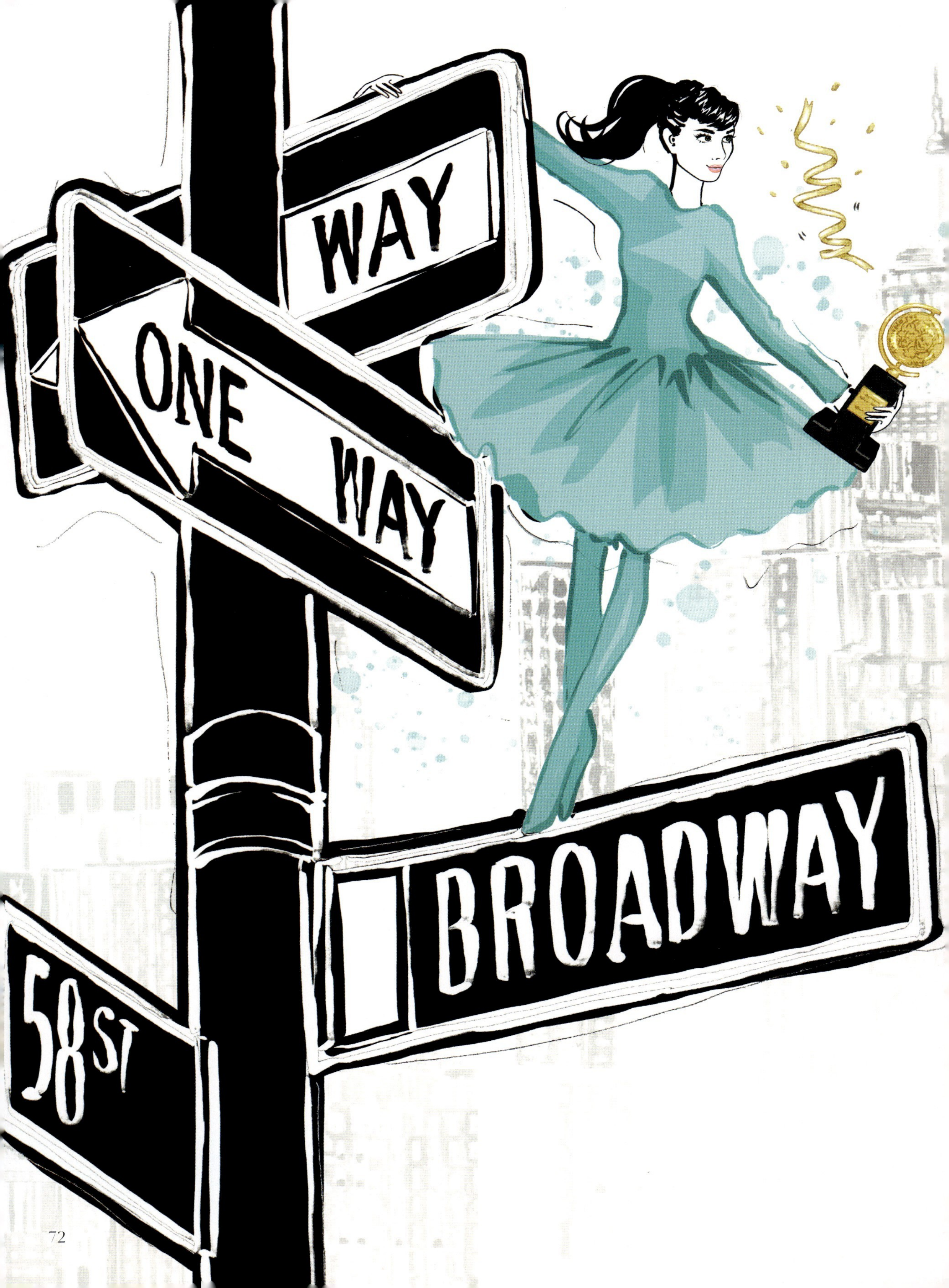
WAY
ONE WAY
BROADWAY
58 ST

After *Roman Holiday*, Audrey returned to the theatre, where she was cast alongside Mel Ferrer in *Ondine*.

She and Ferrer had been set up by Gregory Peck at a party he hosted in London, and love was blooming. *Ondine* was the first of many projects they would work on together.

The play, a tale of a water sprite who falls in love with a knight, was another huge hit, and its success was credited wholly to Audrey's unique onstage presence.

She went on to win a Tony for her performance.

Audrey also won a raft of awards for *Roman Holiday*, including a Golden Globe, a BAFTA and an Oscar — which she collected wearing a white floral gown by the young French designer Hubert de Givenchy.

By the end of the year, she was on the cover of *Time* magazine.

Having captured people's hearts in record time, she worried about living up to all the hype, once comparing her early awards to being given something as a child that she had to grow into.

But grow into them she did.

Her next big film was *Sabrina* in 1954, and she continued to enchant audiences almost universally.

It was during pre-production for *Sabrina* that she would meet her most important collaborator of all.

Edith Head was once again overseeing the wardrobe for the film. But while the notable designer was to be in charge of the 'before' clothes for Audrey's character – a chauffer's daughter turned Paris sophisticate – the studio gave Audrey leave to source the refined Parisian evening wear for the 'after' looks herself.

Having just spent a large chunk of her *Roman Holiday* pay cheque on a Givenchy coat, Audrey went straight to the fledgling designer's studio in Paris to ask if he would design custom outfits for the film.

Roman Holiday was yet to be released so Audrey was still relatively unknown. Givenchy was expecting to meet the more famous Katharine Hepburn and was reportedly disappointed when Audrey walked in.

Givenchy was struck by Audrey's 'beautiful eyes, short hair, thick eyebrows, very tiny trousers, ballerina shoes and a little T-shirt'.

Still Givenchy declined her proposal, telling her, 'No, Mademoiselle, I can't dress you.'

But Audrey didn't give up. She chose a series of outfits from the sample racks instead and invited Givenchy to dinner.

By the end of that night, she not only had an Oscar-award-winning wardrobe for *Sabrina*, she had also made a lifelong friend.

Audrey described it
as the moment when
fashion came into her life.

"

GIVENCHY'S clothes are the ONLY ONES I FEEL myself in.

HE IS MORE
than a designer,
HE IS A CREATOR
of personality.

"

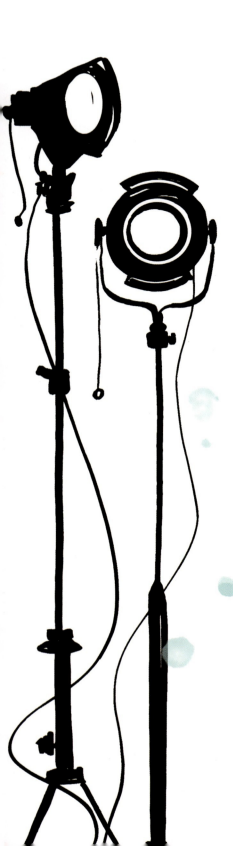

When *Sabrina* was released, magazine *Silver Screen* applauded Audrey's refined look, saying she was 'changing Hollywood's taste'.

The film's French premiere was scheduled for the day after Givenchy's Spring–Summer couture show during 'collections week', and Audrey relished the opportunity to wear her character's couture outfits again for publicity.

The horizontal neckline fastened with a bow at each shoulder would be forever known as the 'Sabrina' neckline.

In an era of stars like Marilyn Monroe and Elizabeth Taylor, Audrey's love for sophisticated simplicity stood out.

Her steadfast refusal to wear
shoulder pads or pad her chest were
revolutionary.

Persistently self-conscious of her
height, her insistence on flat shoes
was equally refreshing.

The fashion world had also started to take notice.

Designers, editors and photographers fell in love with Audrey's refined lines, dancer's sense of physicality and eye for avant-garde silhouettes, and soon she was a regular in *Vogue* and *Harper's Bazaar*.

When it came time to cast *Funny Face*, a musical tale of a fashion editor looking for the next big trend, Audrey was the obvious choice to play unlikely model Jo Stockton.

Again, the costumes for the film were overseen by Edith Head, but this time Audrey insisted that Givenchy design all her outfits.

The result was one of the most important films in fashion history. From Jo dancing in a black turtleneck and cigarette pants, to her walking down the steps of the Louvre in a strapless Givenchy gown, each look was more memorable than the last.

The role was a huge deal for Audrey, as it gave her the opportunity to dance alongside Fred Astaire, a childhood hero of hers, on the streets of Paris.

Astaire's character, Dick Avery, was loosely based on Richard Avedon, one of the most influential photographers of the day, who had built his career on the back of photographing Christian Dior's revolutionary New Look.

Avedon played a consulting role in the shooting of the film, and, in a case of art imitating life, Audrey was already his real-life muse.

Her first cover with him was for *Harper's Bazaar*'s April 1956 edition, and throughout her career the pair would collaborate often.

Their most important work together
was a twenty-page sequence called 'Paris
Pursuit' for *Harper's Bazaar* in 1959.

Audrey once said that working with
Avedon was like having a conversation
with a good friend.

Avedon was equally gushing: 'I am and
forever will be devastated by the gift of
Audrey Hepburn before my camera.
I cannot lift her to greater heights.'

"

I NEVER THINK
of myself as
AN ICON.
I just do my thing.

"

The work kept coming. Audrey took seminal roles in *A Nun's Story*, for which she received another Oscar nomination, and as Natasha in King Vidor's epic adaptation of *War and Peace*, which would take her back to Rome for filming.

Audrey loved spending time in the Italian capital, and the Romans adopted her as one of their own. She returned often to Hotel Hassler when she wasn't working, and the paparazzi regularly captured her strolling the streets, impeccably dressed at all times.

But life wasn't without trials.

In 1954, Audrey had married Mel Ferrer at a ceremony in Switzerland, and while the couple were constantly together, often working on the same projects, they were trying unsuccessfully to start a family.

Audrey suffered two miscarriages during this time, one shortly after falling off a horse and breaking her back while filming the 1960 western *The Unforgiven*.

She also had ongoing contract obligations as part of Hollywood's relentless studio system and on multiple occasions succumbed to severe exhaustion due to her heavy workload.

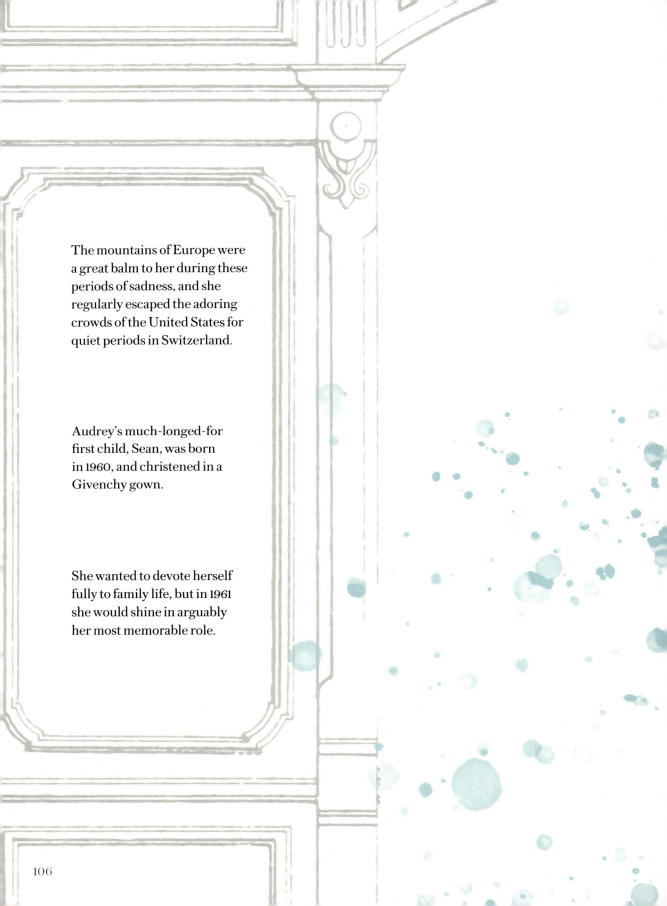

The mountains of Europe were a great balm to her during these periods of sadness, and she regularly escaped the adoring crowds of the United States for quiet periods in Switzerland.

Audrey's much-longed-for first child, Sean, was born in 1960, and christened in a Givenchy gown.

She wanted to devote herself fully to family life, but in 1961 she would shine in arguably her most memorable role.

"

I BELIEVE,
every day, you
SHOULD HAVE
at least one
EXQUISITE
moment.

"

Audrey as Holly Golightly is so indelibly etched in the minds of movie fans, it's incredible to think that her casting was controversial at the time.

But *Breakfast at Tiffany's* author Truman Capote thought she was far too refined to play his eccentric callgirl and instead wanted Marilyn Monroe for the role.

Happily, director Blake Edwards was set on Audrey, and she worked with Givenchy and Edith Head again to bring to life one of the most iconic characters of all time.

The two little black dresses Givenchy designed for Holly Golightly are still endlessly referenced in fashion and film today. The first was the full-length sheath dress from the opening scene, the second a shorter version with frills at the hem.

Audrey even managed to look stylish in Holly's more dishevelled scenes, devised by Edith Head. Only she could look sophisticated clad in a men's shirt and satin eye mask, tasselled earplugs hanging from her ears.

The film was released to great
critical and commercial acclaim,
and Audrey was again nominated
for an Oscar.

Even today, the image of her in a
black Givenchy gown and big
sunglasses, hair in a chignon and
cigarette holder in hand, is the visual
shorthand for New York chic.

> "
>
> # LIFE IS A PARTY.
> ## Dress for it.
>
> "

The 1964 film *My Fair Lady* was one of Audrey's other unforgettable roles, forever remembered for the Ascot Dress by costume designer Cecil Beaton.

Beaton was also a brilliant portrait photographer on staff at *Vogue* and spent two days photographing Audrey as Eliza Doolittle, taking over 350 stills.

Like Richard Avedon, Beaton adored working with Audrey, saying that she owed a large debt to her days as a dancer for the way she moved before the camera.

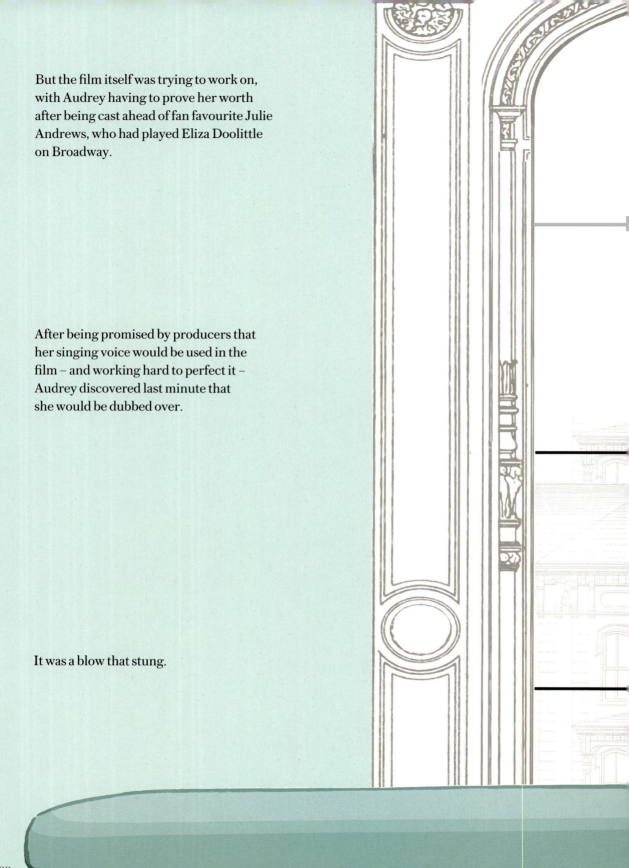

But the film itself was trying to work on, with Audrey having to prove her worth after being cast ahead of fan favourite Julie Andrews, who had played Eliza Doolittle on Broadway.

After being promised by producers that her singing voice would be used in the film – and working hard to perfect it – Audrey discovered last minute that she would be dubbed over.

It was a blow that stung.

In 1963 Audrey had been nominated for a Golden Globe for her role alongside Cary Grant in *Charade*. But the shine was coming off her relationship with the film industry and she didn't like being away from Sean when she was filming.

After seeing out her final obligations with a few more films under contract, including *Wait Until Dark* and *How to Steal a Million*, Audrey made the call to retire in 1967, taking on work only occasionally in the years that followed.

Audrey's friendship with Givenchy endured beyond the end of her film career.

She relied heavily on him as a friend and confidante, and the great designer felt exactly the same way about her.

In 1957 Givenchy had created
a special perfume, L'Interdit,
in honour of their friendship.

When he gifted it to Audrey,
she was so embarrassed by the
special recognition that she
forbade him from selling it.

L'INTERDIT
GIVENCHY

He only acquiesced to a point, saying she could have it to herself for a year before it would be available to the public.

In time, Audrey agreed to be the face of the scent, but she would never accept it as a gift, instead buying it retail for the rest of her life.

Audrey would continue to wear Givenchy's
designs for personal engagements.

When she married her second husband,
the Italian psychiatrist Andrea Dotti – whom
she had met on a Mediterranean cruise in
1968 – she wore a knee-length Givenchy dress
in ballet pink with matching headscarf.

Audrey had her second son,
Luca, with Dotti in 1970.

At the time she turned her back on Hollywood, Audrey was an actor at the height of her career.

She had five Academy Award nominations, including the win for *Roman Holiday*, three BAFTAs and two Golden Globes, not to mention a roster of famous friends around the globe.

But all she wanted was a normal life with her family.

Audrey appeared in her last film,
Steven Spielberg's *Always*, in 1989,
but by then she was already occupied
with a far more important role.

"

TRUE BEAUTY
in a woman is
REFLECTED IN
her soul.
IT'S THE CARING
that she lovingly gives,

THE PASSION
that she shows,
AND THE BEAUTY
of a woman only
GROWS WITH
passing years.

"

THE
LEGACY

WHEN SHE STEPPED AWAY from the film industry, Audrey was renowned for her style and grace, and had built an astonishing portfolio of classic films that would be referenced and adored for generations.

However, her third act would take her far away from the world of film and fashion and see her leaving the most important legacy of all. From 1988 to 1993 she travelled the world as a UN Goodwill Ambassador, using her extraordinary reach to repay the charity she received in her youth and become an unwavering advocate for children everywhere. She also dedicated herself to her family and found the life that she'd always wanted at an eighteenth-century farmhouse in a small Swiss village.

By the time of her death in 1993, the list of awards next to her name didn't just include Golden Globes and Academy Awards but also the Presidential Medal for Freedom and countless other humanitarian awards. The world lost a Hollywood icon and a great friend to those in need, but Audrey's legacy lives on in so many ways.

Audrey's desire to work beyond
films had been sparked years
earlier while she worked on
A Nun's Story in 1959.

In preparation for that role, she
had spent time observing nuns in
European convents and struck up
a friendship with Marie-Louise
Habets, the inspiration for the film.

She spoke of it being a
transformative experience.

She had also served as a volunteer nurse in a Dutch hospital as a teenager in the years after the war. She had tended to a wounded paratrooper named Terence Young and, remarkably, towards the end of her career had been reunited with him when he directed her in *Wait Until Dark*.

Stepping back from work to look after her sons was in some ways a continuation of Audrey's mission to care for others.

Motherhood was the thing she cared about most in life, and she was dedicated to raising her children away from the glare of the camera.

The family spent a decade living in her beloved city of Rome, and her sons spoke of happy times growing up there with a mother who revelled in the smaller details: cooking, walking her dogs and taking her boys to school.

In 1964 Audrey had also bought a home in the quiet village of Tolochenaz in Switzerland. She had said that all she had dreamed of as a child was a house with a garden, not huge luxuries, and this is what she found at 'La Paisible'.

The eighteenth-century stone farmhouse was surrounded by farms, fruit orchards and vineyards and had a huge vegetable garden.

"
TO PLANT
a garden
IS TO BELIEVE
in tomorrow.
"

In 1980 Audrey met her final partner,
Robert Wolders, a Dutch actor who had
spent the war years in the Netherlands,
only an hour from Arnhem.

Their time together in
Tolochenaz was one of the
happiest periods of her life.

Yet as she neared sixty, Audrey was ready for something new. And her next big break would come when UNICEF asked her to become a Goodwill Ambassador in 1988.

Driven by her memories of Arnhem and a 'long-lasting gratitude and trust for what UNICEF does' for children after having received food and medical relief from them herself, she threw herself into the role with determination.

After decades of a slower-paced life, Audrey was back to a schedule of constant travel and long hours, determined to go wherever she could bring attention to an issue.

Her first trip was to Ethiopia, where drought and conflict had led to famine.

In the following years she visited war-torn countries, humanitarian disaster zones and places of flood, drought and disease in order to shine a spotlight on the corners of the world that needed help.

In the days of movie promotions, Audrey had agreed to only three or four interviews a day, but for UNICEF she would return home from field trips and book ten or fifteen commitments a day to talk about the causes she was passionate about.

She was deeply committed to the organisation and worked tirelessly to convince the world that the welfare of children was the world's most solemn responsibility.

Whenever someone expressed admiration for her work, she would dismiss them, insisting that it was a great privilege.

Friends tried to convince her to slow down at times, but she wouldn't hear of it.

She took the same attitude when she fell ill on a trip to Somalia in 1992 with terrible stomach pains, refusing to return home early. Some say she was unwell even before the trip but refused her doctors' calls to get tests lest it interfere with her work.

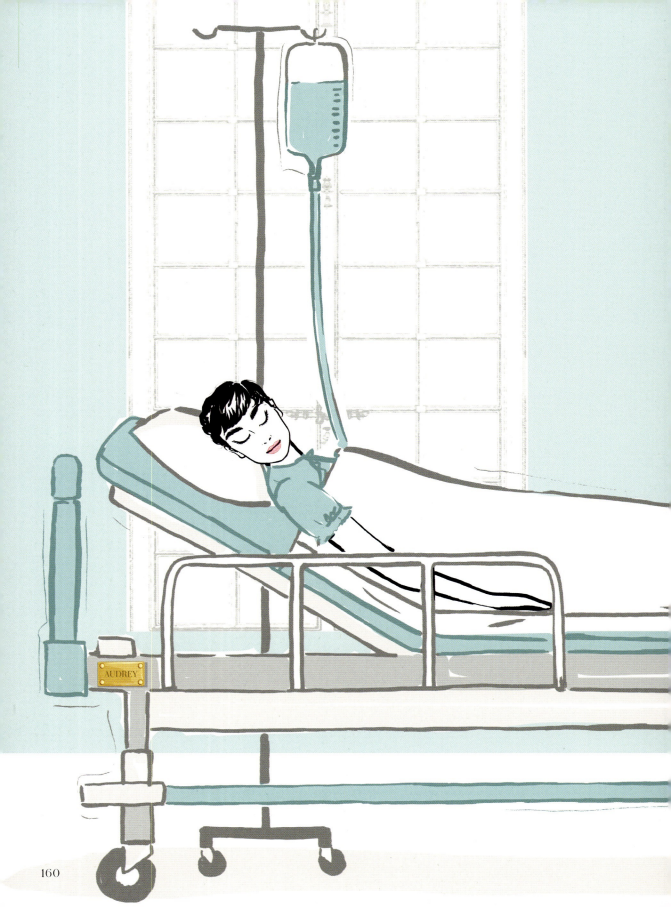

Back in the United States, Audrey had tests that led to a diagnosis of appendiceal cancer.

She had surgery almost immediately, but her health deteriorated quickly.

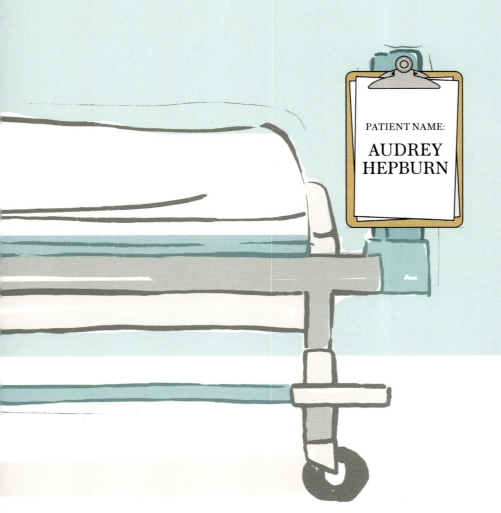

PATIENT NAME:

AUDREY HEPBURN

By December Audrey was too unwell to attend the presentation of the award for the US Presidential Medal of Freedom, the country's highest civilian honour.

She was desperate to
return to La Paisible for
a last Christmas with
family and friends.

When doctors told her she was too ill to take a commercial flight, Givenchy arranged for a private plane to take her instead, filling it with roses for the journey.

"

HOW SHALL
I sum up my life?
I THINK I'VE BEEN
particularly lucky.

"

Audrey died at La Paisible on
20 January 1993, less than three
months after her initial diagnosis.

The world mourned a star,
a mother, a friend and a
humanitarian champion.

Villagers lined the streets for her funeral
in Tolochenaz, and she was buried in a
simple plot near the shores of Lac Leman
that is now covered in flowers.

AUDREY
HEPBURN

20. 01. 1993

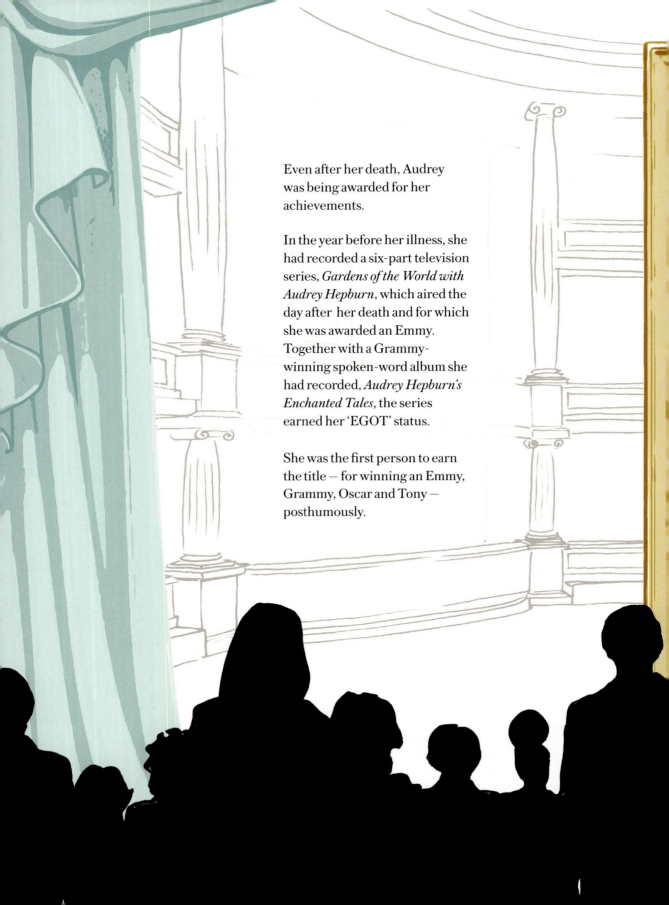

Even after her death, Audrey was being awarded for her achievements.

In the year before her illness, she had recorded a six-part television series, *Gardens of the World with Audrey Hepburn*, which aired the day after her death and for which she was awarded an Emmy. Together with a Grammy-winning spoken-word album she had recorded, *Audrey Hepburn's Enchanted Tales*, the series earned her 'EGOT' status.

She was the first person to earn the title — for winning an Emmy, Grammy, Oscar and Tony — posthumously.

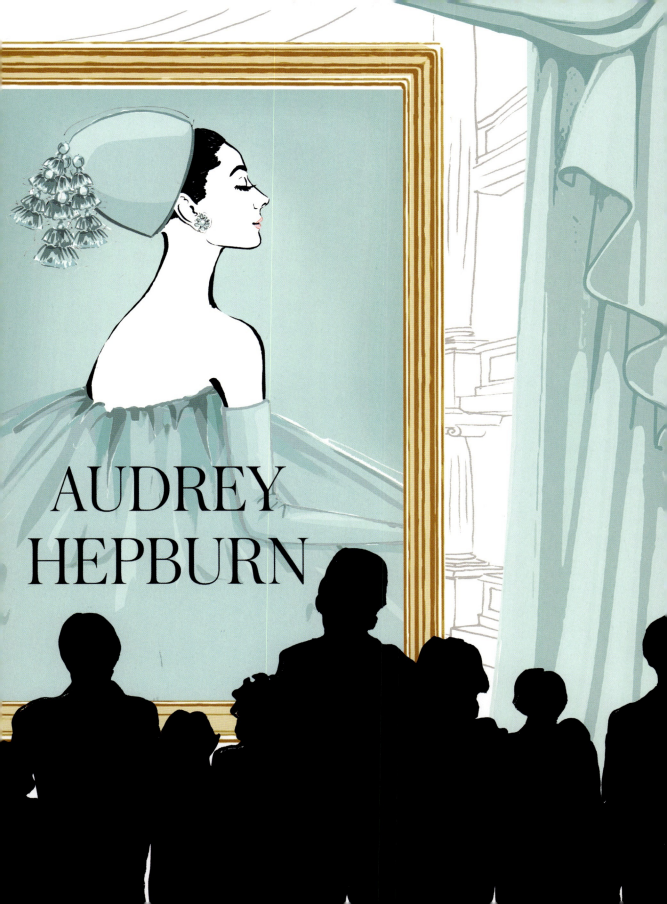

AUDREY
HEPBURN

Audrey was also posthumously awarded
the Jean Hersholt Humanitarian Award,
her final Oscar statuette, which was
presented by none other than long-time
friend Gregory Peck.

Her legacy of love lives on in
her sons. Luca runs the Audrey
Hepburn Children's Fund, while
Sean is the honorary chair of
The Audrey Hepburn Society
at the US Fund for UNICEF.

AUDREY
HEPBURN

173

Even today, her movies remain timeless.

Her characters are as contemporary as they were when she conceived of them. Her image is still perhaps the most recognisable of all Hollywood stars, and her photographs hang in galleries everywhere.

Throughout her life, Audrey maintained her unparalleled gift for dressing and was renowned for turning every outfit into a classic look.

Her personal uniform of a simple t-shirt, cropped pants and short hair was the very definition of chic, and her incredible film looks are endlessly imitated.

Cecil Beaton once observed of Audrey Hepburn that 'nobody ever looked like her before World War II. Now thousands of imitations have appeared'.

"

WITH HAIR
tied in a bun,
BIG SUNGLASSES
and black dress,
EVERY WOMAN
can look like me.

"

Her fashion legacy will forever be tied to Givenchy. Audrey considered him her life's 'great love'.

Givenchy visited her that final Christmas for one last stroll around her beloved garden. As he was preparing to leave, Audrey presented him with a navy blue quilted coat.

'Think of me when you wear it,' she told him.

Even decades later, the memory would bring tears to the designer's eyes. 'From Geneva to Paris I wept in the jacket she had given me,' he remembered.

In 2014, Givenchy created a retrospective of their work together, 'To Audrey with Love', which paid tribute to the fashion world's greatest platonic romance.

When Givenchy and Audrey began their collaboration, there were no Hollywood actors who had such an intimate partnership with a designer.

They had pioneered something special.

Givenchy would later say of Audrey, 'she was an enchantress, inspiring love and beauty, and fairies never quite disappear altogether'.

As a young girl in war-torn Arnhem, Audrey could never have imagined where life would take her, but the world can be forever grateful that she shared her journey with so many.

In her own words, 'Living is like tearing through a museum.

'Not until later do you really start absorbing what you saw, thinking about it, looking it up in a book, and remembering – because you can't take it in all at once.'

"

FOR BEAUTIFUL
eyes, look for the
GOOD IN OTHERS;
for beautiful lips,
SPEAK ONLY
words of kindness;

AND FOR POISE, walk with the KNOWLEDGE that you are NEVER ALONE.

"

ACKNOWLEDGEMENTS

To Emily Hart and Arwen Summers for stepping into the world of Audrey and creating such a beautiful book with me.

To Martina Granolic, thank you for diving head first into Audrey's life and for painstakingly piecing every single moment of her journey together. We swooned over her iconic fashion and we even shed a few tears discovering the depths of her humanitarian work.

To Andrea Davison for so beautifully researching and crafting everything wonderful about Audrey's incredible life. As always, you found so many fascinating details that brought such depth to her story.

To Murray Batten, our ninth book together! Thank you for creating such a beautiful and elegant design to house Audrey's story. Every single page is designed to perfection.

To Todd Rechner for your incredible care and attention in seeing my books to their finished form. You've made each book something precious to hold, to read, to keep forever. Thank you.

To Justine Clay for first discovering my work and setting me on my way. I am forever grateful to have met you.

To my husband Craig and my children Gwyn and Will, thank you for letting my Audrey obsession into our life. I can't promise I won't watch *Breakfast at Tiffany's* one more time!

ABOUT THE AUTHOR

Megan Hess was destined to draw. An initial career in graphic design evolved into art direction for some of the world's leading advertising agencies and for Liberty London. In 2008, Megan illustrated Candace Bushnell's number-one-bestselling book *Sex and the City*. This catapulted Megan onto the world stage, and she began illustrating portraits for *The New York Times*, *Vogue Italia*, *Vanity Fair* and *TIME*, who described Megan's work as 'love at first sight'.

Today, Megan is one of the world's most sought-after fashion illustrators, with a client list that includes Givenchy, Tiffany & Co., Valentino, Louis Vuitton and *Harper's Bazaar*. Megan's iconic style has been used in global campaigns for Fendi, Prada, Cartier, Dior and Salvatore Ferragamo. She has illustrated live for fashion shows such as Fendi at Milan Fashion Week, Chopard at the 2019 Cannes Film Festival, Viktor&Rolf and Christian Dior Couture.

Megan has created a signature look for Bergdorf Goodman, New York, and a bespoke bag collection for Harrods of London. She has illustrated a series of portraits for Michelle Obama, as well as portraits for Gwyneth Paltrow, Cate Blanchett and Nicole Kidman. She is also the Global Artist in Residence for the prestigious Oetker Hotel Collection.

Megan illustrates all her work with a custom Montblanc pen that she affectionately calls 'Monty'.

Megan has written and illustrated nine bestselling fashion books, as well as her much-loved series for children, Claris the Chicest Mouse in Paris.

When she's not in her studio working, you'll find her watching *Breakfast at Tiffany's* for the hundredth time, dreaming of croissants and Givenchy couture.

Visit Megan at meganhess.com

Published in 2022 by Hardie Grant Books,
an imprint of Hardie Grant Publishing

Hardie Grant Books (Melbourne)
Building 1, 658 Church Street
Richmond, Victoria 3121

Hardie Grant Books (London)
5th & 6th Floors
52–54 Southwark Street
London SE1 1UN

hardiegrantbooks.com

A catalogue record for this
book is available from the
National Library of Australia

Audrey Hepburn
ISBN 978 1 74379 836 2

10 9 8 7 6 5 4 3 2 1

Publisher: Arwen Summers
Project Editor: Emily Hart
Researcher: Andrea Davison
Designer: Murray Batten
Production Manager: Todd Rechner
Design Manager: Kristin Thomas
Production Coordinator: Jessica Harvie

Colour reproduction by Splitting Image Colour Studio
Printed in China by Leo Paper Products LTD.

The paper this book is printed on is from FSC®-certified
forests and other sources. FSC® promotes environmentally
responsible, socially beneficial and economically viable
management of the world's forests.

Hardie Grant acknowledges the Traditional Owners of the country on which we work,
the Wurundjeri people of the Kulin nation and the Gadigal people of the Eora nation,
and recognises their continuing connection to the land, waters and culture. We pay our
respects to their Elders past, present and emerging.